This book belongs to:

Presented to:

____

From:

____

40 Days to Spiritual Reset

Rediscovering Your Passion for God While Serving in His Vineyard

IEASHA M. POWELL

Published by:
CSP Publishing
Kingston, Jamaica

ISBN: 978 976 96721 1 6

Cover Design by: Ieasha M. Powell
Interior Design by: Ieasha M. Powell

To my husband, Christopher, for always being my loudest cheerleader

Acknowledgement

During the process of writing this devotional, many things have happened. Things that could easily break any man or woman, depending on where they are in their spiritual journey. It's in times like these when you are pouring out your heart that the enemy comes to ruin things. But I have overcome! I've finished the task at hand!

It would be remiss of me to pretend I did it on my own, however. I must single out my dearest friend, Terry-Ann Nelson, who has been a tower of strength to me more than she could ever fathom. Your warm presence and constant encouragement afforded me strength even in the darkest times to get through the process of writing this book. Thank you!

To my incredible husband who is my constant support, both in the good and bad times. It's been nine years and you're still the same caring man as you were back then. Thank you for pushing me to let my heart out on paper, even if it doesn't come out right the first, second or third time. Thank you, honey. I love you!

And to all the people in my life who've contributed to my good and bad experiences. Thank you! Your contribution to my growth and development is well appreciated!

Finally, to the only wise God, my Father and King, the Lord Jesus Christ. Thank You for being the best Daddy a girl could ask for!

Table of Contents

Foreword

God's promises are indeed true for His children. As the word of God says in James 1:17, "Every good gift and every perfect gift is from above, and cometh down from the Father of lights, with whom is no variableness, neither shadow of turning."

When my friend, Ieasha, reached out to me for feedback on her book, I was more than happy to, knowing that she is a gifted writer with a profound desire to share her thoughts with the world through her writing. As I went through the book, "40 Days to Spiritual Reset," I quickly realized what a goldmine I had in my hand! Immediately, I started using the devotional pieces in my own daily devotion. The entries are not only easy to read and understand, but also filled with biblical truths that every Christian needs to hear.

Truly, there are days when we feel down and out as Christians. The desire to fast and pray is just not there, especially when the many trials that have come to try us, begins to wreak havoc in our lives. Sometimes we just need that extra push to get back in the game, and 40 Days to Spiritual Reset is just the book to get you there. I love that I am able to get up in the mornings and not worry about what to read for that day. In the book, there is a focus scripture provided, as well as a one page read to help align your thoughts for prayer and supplication. There is also space provided for you to answer the questions asked of you, as well as any other thoughts you may deem relevant in your devotion session.

The stories shared are real, beautiful and uniquely parallel with varying themes of scripture. I guarantee that this book will renew your faith in God through encouragement mixed with biblical truth pills we all need in our walk with our Lord Jesus Christ. Nothing is more important than our covenant relationship with the Lord. Martha, when she complained to Jesus about her sister, Mary, not helping her to do the work, the Lord told her, "… Mary hath chosen that good part, which shall not be taken away from her." Reference: Luke 10:40-42

Too many times, we are more focused on the work of the Lord instead of our relationship with the Lord, as the author so eloquently points out in this book. 40 Days to Spiritual Reset is here to guide you back into that needed covenant relationship with Christ, with clear and precise instructions to reach your goal. 40 days, I believe, is a perfect time for a reset, a refreshing, a renewal. Jesus fasted for 40 days and 40 nights before he went into ministry. Even our Lord prepared Himself for what was to come.

When was the last time you fasted? Or prayed? And I mean really prayed? Are you no longer excited about reading the Word of God? If your responses to these questions are in the negative, then 40 Days to Spiritual Reset is just the book for you. Without reservation, I give it my full recommendation!

Mrs. Terry-Ann Nelson
Resource Personnel and Sunday School Teacher - Sunday School Department; Children Church Ministry
Pentecostal Sanctuary UPC

*[12]For we wrestle not against flesh and blood, but against
principalities, against powers, against the rulers of the darkness
of this world, against spiritual wickedness in high places.*
Ephesians 6:12

Introduction

Spirituality, much like love, is a word that has been overused and abused in every nook and crevice of society. People who once denied the existence of the spirit realm, now talk about it as much as Christians do, perhaps more. Thanks to gurus on the internet and their "self-help" books, many people have found what they call, "enlightenment," and claim to be freer and happier than they've ever been before.

This should be a good thing, right? Acknowledgement and exploration of the spirit realm should bring people to an awareness of God and His righteousness. Should. Unfortunately, this isn't the case. The world has never been further away from God than it is now, despite this *age of enlightenment*. If we were to do a quick online research, we would find that not only is spirituality more popular than ever, but it comes with many paths.

In any online business – freelancing, affiliate marketing, book publishing, blogging, etc. – we will more than likely find a genre for spirituality. Under this genre, you may find sub-genres like hypnosis, astrology, witchcraft, etc.

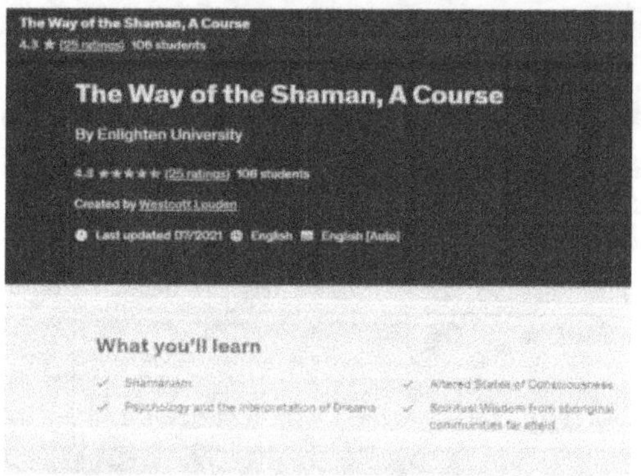

Fig. 1 source: www.udemy.com

If you want to become a witch, spirit guide or shaman, all you have to do is Google courses in these areas, and you are sure to find one! (see Fig. 1 above) This is the kind of world we are living in as Christians. Everyone is now spiritual. They seek to learn more about the spirit realm, except they don't want our Lord and Saviour Jesus Christ mixed into it.

The enemy of our souls, Satan, has effectively turned the minds of people away from God by discrediting spiritual things, only to turn these same people back to the realms of the spirit without any regard for God. Of course, him being a spirit himself, need you and I to connect with him on that level. The problem is, we don't gain spiritual freedom from connecting with Satan, but ultimate bondage, for he only comes to kill, steal and destroy (John 10:10).

Category ∧

Spirituality, New Age & Alternative Beliefs

Astrology (26)

General (116)

Hypnosis (19)

Magic (6)

Numerology (4)

Paranormal (1)

Psychics (19)

Religion (7)

Tarot (9)

Witchcraft (7)

Fig. 2 source: www.fiverr.com

This is why we must be on our guards at all times and avoid listening to people who claim to be spiritual, yet fail to ever mention Jesus Christ in their teachings. Spiritual gurus will use words like **mantra, karma, transcendental meditation, yoga, enlightenment,** etc., to deliver their very convincing message. A quick study of any of these will show that they are all demonic rituals that only entertain darkness and destruction in our lives.

True spiritual freedom can only come through Jesus Christ. Any human being who enters the spirit realm without the Holy Ghost as their spiritual clothing will encounter dark forces that they cannot handle on their own. When Jesus Christ came on the scene in Israel, every demon who sensed Him went on high alert. They did not see a man as others did. They saw a pure and undefiled human spirit wrapped up in the Holy Spirit, a force which they could not withstand.

...Let us alone; what have we to do with thee, thou Jesus of Nazareth? art thou come to destroy us? I know thee who thou art, the Holy One of God. Mark 1:24

The spirit realm is not something to be toyed with, as it may be the difference between life and death, a blessing and a curse. This book is for Christians who desire to be seen in the spirit realm as the holy children of God. Many of us have either made a mess of ourselves in our walk with Christ, or have inherited spiritual curses that have been traveling through our family lineage for ages. Either way, a spiritual reset is in order.

What is a Spiritual Reset?

Think about your Wi-Fi router. Whenever it starts acting up, there is a reset button that you can hit to get it back to working order. Whatever glitch that was in the system preventing it from working properly is erased and now you basically have a clean slate from which to work.

A spiritual reset, though not as simple as pressing a reset button, does give the same result. A clean slate is what we aim for as children of God, for we know that it is impossible for us to enter the kingdom of heaven spotted and blemished. Spiritual compromise comes in many forms. As mentioned before, it may be that you made a mess of things. Perhaps you entered an ungodly relationship that killed your connection with God. Maybe you were stealing while singing on the choir. Or you told some lies you knew you shouldn't have, but did anyway.

Here's another one that affects many young Christians today. Perhaps you've been reading books or watching movies that promote sin and you've become so addicted to them that your relationship with God got severed. I personally have dealt with this so I know it's a real and utterly powerful struggle.

Then there are those curses that come from our earthly connections. Family curses are the most popular among us. While we've repented of our sins, been baptized in the name of Jesus Christ and have received His precious Holy Spirit, there are some things that we never got delivered from. These spiritual forces cling to our lives, following us everywhere we go, and making a ruckus of our very existence at the worst possible moments.

Another possible scenario is this. You may be in the church for years, giving yourself in service to God's work, yet have neglected having a robust relationship with God Himself. Perhaps things started out well with the Lord, but overtime, prayer, fasting and the reading of His word fell through the cracks, leaving you feeling like a mere shell of the Christian you used to be.

Whether you fall into one or more of these categories, it is important that we go into spiritual reset mode. In order to serve God with sincerity and godly passion, we ought to take time out to replenish our relationship with Him.

Whenever my husband and I feel like we need to replenish our relationship, we pull away from our busy schedules, forget about everyone and everything around us, and lock in to each other. We know well enough that life can get so busy that we end up neglecting each other in favour of *getting things done.*

In the same way, we sometimes get caught up with doing the work of the Lord without getting to know the Lord we are working for. Jesus made a chilling declaration in Matthew 7:22-23. He said, "Many will say to me in that day, Lord, Lord, have we not prophesied in thy name? and in thy name have cast out devils? and in thy name done many wonderful works? [23]And then will I profess unto them, I never knew you: depart from me, ye that work iniquity."

Imagine working for the Lord all your life, only to be told by Him that He never knew you! It's an inconceivable thought for many people. But sadly, that is what some will hear on that great day. If one has not taken the time to know the mind of God (His Word) for himself, and carry out His will according to what is written, then this is what he will hear in the end. We cannot claim to be Christians without being familiar with God's plan for us, both individually and collectively.

It is time for us to put things in their proper perspectives. Our relationship with Jesus Christ is more important than anything else in this world, and it is high time that we start treating it as such. Let us get back to basics by locking in with God again through daily devotion.

There is no time to waste because the coming of the Lord is so very near, and soon this world will collapse into more darkness than it has ever seen before. No matter what the world says to try to convince us otherwise, making our calling and election sure, is the most important decision we will ever make in our lives.

How to Reset Spiritually

Simply put, we reset spiritually through the age-old triple punch of fasting, prayer and daily consummation of the Word of God. In order to separate ourselves from the desires of the flesh, we must fast. In order to connect with God, we must pray. And in order to know God's will, we must read His Word. Without these three things, we cannot adequately do a spiritual reset.

This reset will not only rekindle our relationship with God, but will also give us spiritual muscles to fight on a higher level. While we may win some battles in our current state, there are some strongholds that will never be broken unless we fast, pray and read God's word.

19 Then came the disciples to Jesus apart, and said, Why could not we cast him out? 20 And Jesus said unto them, Because of your unbelief: for verily I say unto you, If ye have faith as a grain of mustard seed, ye shall say unto this mountain, Remove hence to yonder place; and it shall remove; and nothing shall be impossible unto you. 21 Howbeit this kind goeth not out but by prayer and fasting. Matthew 17:19-21

Benefits of Prayer, Fasting and Reading God's Word

- We develop a closer relationship with God
- We become more aware of how the spirit realm works and how to navigate through it.
- Our faith in God increases
- Our passion for the Word is rekindled
- Our desire for the world lessens.
- We start to see everything around us through the eyes of God
- We gain power and authority over vile demons that we otherwise could not have handled before.
- We develop the fruit of the spirit, which brings us to perfection in God.
- We gain healing from varying sicknesses and diseases plaguing the mind and body.

Fasting

Fasting is abstaining from food for the purpose of disciplining the flesh and connecting to God on a deeper spiritual level. Fasting has been practiced for thousands of years, not only by godly people, but also those who seek other spiritual mediums as we mentioned earlier. To some, it may seem like self-inflicting starvation, but in reality, it brings more power than the human mind can comprehend.

Most, if not all of us, struggle to stay away from something. People usually equate lack of self-control to sexual sins or short-temperedness, but it goes so much deeper than that. Watching too much TV, spending your hard-earned money every month on things you don't need, or eating too much of that treat you love so much, are all issues that stem from a lack of self-control. As I write this, I can recall those times when I've binge watched a couple of tele-series that I'd become addicted to. Even when my eyes were tired and I needed sleep, I kept telling myself, "Just one more episode and then I'm done," only to find myself clicking the next one, and then the next one, until the sun starts peeking over the horizon.

Some of us would never do drugs and often feel this grave weight of disappointment toward those who allow it to control their lives. Yet, we never consider that there are things in our lives that control us as well. Whether it be food, shopping, social media or watching our favourite tele-series, over-indulgence is a sin in God's sight.

By restricting ourselves from getting what we crave the most, we are bringing our human desires under control. Once our flesh is under control, the Spirit can rule. The Bible teaches us in Galatians 5:17, "...the flesh lusteth against the Spirit, and the Spirit against the flesh: and these are contrary the one to the other: so that ye cannot do the things that ye would." The flesh is an enemy to the spirit. Thus, it must be put under subjection.

Biblical Types of Fast:

- Standard Fast: e.g. Jesus' Fast – Jesus abstained from food completely. He only drank water.

- Partial Fast: e.g. Daniel's Fast – Daniel ate vegetables and drank water during his fast. He did not eat calorically dense foods like fish and meats.

- Absolute Fast: eg. Moses and Paul - In Exodus 34:28, it is recorded that Moses did not eat or drink anything for forty days and forty nights while on Mount Sinai. Also, in Acts 9:9, Paul the Apostle did not eat or drink as he waited for Ananias to come to him.

Fasting is a biblical principle that surrounds abstinence from food. Nevertheless, it is important that we stay away from other forms of pleasure during our time of consecration. Fasting in scripture equates to mourning or suffering. We cannot indulge ourselves in any kind of pleasure when we are working toward bringing the body under subjection. As such, we must also go through an abstinence fast.

Abstinence Fast goes beyond food. It also includes staying away from:

- Sex
- Television
- Social Media
- Long Telephone Conversations
- In appropriate or unnecessary reading material
- And just about anything you struggle with.

Why Forty (40) Days for a Reset?

Forty (40), as represented in scripture, is the numerical value used for periods of judgment, trial, preparation and even new beginnings.

In Genesis 7, God sent rain upon the earth 40 days and nights, because wickedness had permeated the land and needed to be cleansed. Noah and his family were the only ones spared from this **judgment**. After those 40 days of judgment, **new life** began.

Numbers 14: 33 and Joshua 5:6, it is recorded that the children of Israel were forced to roam the wilderness for 40 years because they did not belief God's promises or obey His word. As such, they all died in the wilderness, saving the young ones who would have become the next generation after them. This was God's **judgment** on the nation. The next generation represented a **new beginning**.

In Deuteronomy 25:1-3, the children of Israel are instructed that if a man is found to be wicked in a matter, his punishment must not exceed 40 stripes, as this will make the **judge** seem to despise his brother who is being punished.

As recorded in Matthew 4:2, Mark 1:13 and Luke 4:2, Jesus was led by the Spirit into the wilderness, where he was **tried** by the tempter, Satan. This was part of His **preparation** for ministry.

In ancient Hebrew society, we see where Hebrew men would take a wife at 40 (Isaac - Genesis 25:20; Esau - Genesis 26:34). 40 represents a **new generation**.

A 40 day reset is ideal for the purpose of laying ourselves at the feet of the Lord Jesus and asking for a renewal, a refreshing, and a revival. It is necessary for a period of repentance, trial, preparation and new beginnings that will bring us well needed transformation.

The fasting schedule that you choose during this period is all up to you. As mentioned earlier, biblical fasts include:

- a standard fast in which you have only water for your forty days of reset

- a partial fast in which you consume only vegetables and water, or

- an absolute fast, in which you consume nothing. Please be advised that going more than three or four days without water may cause extreme dehydration. If you choose to do this fast, please do it at three-day intervals.

Thank you for being a part of this journey with me! We can and will achieve spiritual victory, if we only but commit ourselves to the work needed. I pray that everything you've put before the Lord during this season of reset will bring answers according to God's will and purpose for your life.

Happy reset!

Pray without ceasing!!!
1 Thessalonians 5:17
Thy word is a lamp unto my feet, and a light unto my path!!!
Psalm 119:105
Therefore also now, saith the Lord, turn ye even to me with all your heart, and with fasting, and with weeping, and with mourning:
Joel 2:12

Day 1 - What's Your Passion?

Scripture: [1]*As the hart panteth after the water brooks, so panteth my soul after thee, O God.* Psalm 42:1

Passion is an element of human emotion that can be considered intense, deep, nearly out of control. It can be negative or positive. Most of us have, at some point in our lives, experienced passion. Passion for art. Passion for family. Passion for friends. Passion for education. Passion for success. Passion for that man or woman. The question now is, do we have that same zealous passion toward God?

David, in the Psalms, had that intense passion for God. He was on a desperate hunt to get closer and closer to God. Despite all his failings, and there were many, he was referred to as a man after God's own heart, simply because of where his passion lay.

As we enter into this spiritual reset, let us each examine our hearts. Do you have that deep driving force that David had towards God? Or do you find yourself losing interest in prayer, fasting and reading God's word? Are you struggling to connect with God on a deeper level? And finally, are you distracted by temporal things to the point where you've forgotten to focus on the spiritual things that connect you to God?

This self-assessment will give us insight into where our deepest passions lie, thereby giving us a full understanding of where we fall short in our walk with the Lord Jesus. Write down the answer to each of the questions above and put them before the Lord in prayer. The only way to fix the breaches is to acknowledge that they exist in the first place!

So come, let's assess!

A prayer: *Lord Jesus, help me to rediscover my passion in You and for You. Like King David, Your servant, give me that deep desire to be closer and closer to You. In Jesus' name, Amen.*

Notes

Day 2 – Choosing God

Scripture: *²⁴No man can serve two masters: for either he will hate the one, and love the other; or else he will hold to the one, and despise the other. Ye cannot serve God and mammon.* Matthew 6:24

Choices. We make them on a daily basis. Be they simple or great, they form the backbone of how our day turns out. If you choose to drive a different route to work to avoid traffic, you may end up getting to work early like you wanted. Then again, you may very well find that the route is just as congested, perhaps more, which defeats the purpose of changing routes. You're still late for work. That's the power of choices.

Jesus gave a clear message in Matthew 6:24. You cannot serve God and mammon (money). Paul also declares in 1 Timothy 6:10, *For the love of money is the root of all evil: which while some coveted after, they have erred from the faith, and pierced themselves through with many sorrows.*

How many times have we seen some of our church leaders turn a blind eye to some vile things their wealthy members do, simply to not lose the mammon? Despite Jesus' words in Luke 12:15, we still treat the rich like kings and the poor like peasants. While we are reconnecting with God, we must remember that in order to serve the Lord Jesus, we must be willing to walk away from filthy lucre. We must not be afraid to speak the truth, even in the face of powerful men. Choose to serve God, not the mammon!

If you have ever fallen into this state of treating the rich better than the poor, it's not too late to make a change. Write down where you have failed in this endeavour, and put it before the Lord. He is waiting for you with open arms.

A prayer: *Lord Jesus, we have failed to glorify You by despising the poor and elevating the rich. Teach us to walk away from the mammon, and choose to do the right thing always. Amen.*

Notes

Day 3 – Struggling with God

Scripture: *[10]He hath destroyed me on every side, and I am gone: and mine hope hath he removed like a tree.* Job 19:10

Nobody likes to struggle. As human beings, we enjoy having a smooth and easy life without glitches. Yet, that's a fantasy world that even the most privileged don't live in. Life is filled with struggles. We cannot get away from them. We shouldn't try to either, because they are what train us and fortify us to become productive people in society.

But what if our struggles were brought on by God's interference? What if the suffering you are facing right now was ordained by God for you to go through? Does this make Him any less desirable in your eyes?

In the famous story of Job, we find that God confidently allowed Satan to torment Job. The wicked one was convinced that he could make Job curse God and die, but Job held on, despite having to do battle with the very people who should have been his support system. I'm persuaded to believe that if it had been me in that situation, I would have given up long before my skin started falling off my body. Yet, we never know the strength that God has placed within us, until that moment when pain and suffering come knocking on our doors.

It is a fact that suffering will come. The Apostles of Christ went through it. Our church fathers throughout the ages went through it. Many are going through it right now, and more will go through it in the future. In order to reign with Christ, we must have a made-up mind to stand with Him, suffer with Him and even to die for Him. Are you ready?

A prayer: *Father, help us to know Your will and to pursue it, even when we suffer for it. Some of us are struggling with the pain. Lend us Your strength, Lord. We need it. We need You. In Jesus' holy name, Amen.*

Notes

Day 4 – The Shiny Object

Scripture: *²⁰And Achan answered Joshua, and said, Indeed I have sinned against the Lord God of Israel, and thus and thus have I done: ²¹When I saw among the spoils a goodly Babylonish garment, and two hundred shekels of silver, and a wedge of gold of fifty shekels weight, then I coveted them, and took them; and, behold, they are hid in the earth in the midst of my tent, and the silver under it.* Joshua 7:20-21

We love shiny things. No matter what race, culture or religion we're from, people tend to go googly-eyed over the sparkle. Wars have been fought throughout history over shiny things. Millions have been murdered, simply because the murderers needed to get their hands on the gold, the silver, the precious stones.

In the story of Achan, we find Israel losing a battle against a small nation, simply because of one man's covetousness for the shiny object. Similarly, Gehazi, in 2 Kings 5, coveted Naaman's shiny things, resulting in him being plagued with Naaman's leprosy.

Today, the shiny object may not be precious jewels or expensive garments. However, there are some opportunities that come to us that didn't come from God. Perhaps you were offered a deal but you know God is not in it. Whatever the shiny object, we must examine our own hearts to see where we've fallen short. The riches of this life have the power to blind us, and make us lose sight of where our affection must lay.

Have you been negotiating deals with the devil lately? What is that sparkly object that's distracting you from giving yourself completely to the will of God? Make a note of it and put it before the Lord.

A prayer: *Lord Jesus, help us to resist the shiny objects and not be consumed with covetousness. May we find contentment in the things that You have blessed us with, in Jesus' name, Amen.*

Notes

Day 5 – In Need of Realignment

Scripture: *Ye do the deeds of your father. Then said they to him, We be not born of fornication; we have one Father, even God.* John 8:41

Have you ever been caught in a conflict that was rigged against you from the start? You know, those ones where you were approached, challenged and then shamed for your points of view on the matter being discussed? It's one of those situations that, if you are not strong emotionally, you may break in front of your adversaries, despite being in the right. Standing on your own with hardened faces surrounding you does not invoke the best feeling in the world.

Jesus had this same experience with the Pharisees, except, He was not afraid to tell them the truth, even though he knew full well they were secretly planning to murder him. The Pharisees were the religious order of the day. They expected everyone to listen to *them* and do *their* bidding. Then the carpenter's son came on the scene and crashed the party. Jesus exposed them for who they were and did all he could to show them, and all of Israel, the true path to righteousness. The Pharisees and their countrymen were in dire need of realignment, but they just couldn't see the path Jesus was setting for them. They resisted him at every turn.

Many of us also struggle to see God's path for our lives. We live in an era where everyone thinks they know, even when they know nothing. Thus, they end up missing out on the truth of God which is well able to save their souls from destruction. Today, let's put our stubborn will aside and realign ourselves with what God desires from us. Write a letter to Jesus. Tell him where you need to be realigned to be fully converted into His own image.

A prayer: *Lord Jesus, teach us to let go of our ideals, our thoughts, our will, and be realigned according to Your will, in Jesus' name, Amen.*

Notes

Day 6 – The Decision-Making Process

Scripture: *²And he said, Take now thy son, thine only son Isaac, whom thou lovest, and get thee into the land of Moriah; and offer him there for a burnt offering upon one of the mountains which I will tell thee of.* Genesis 22:2

What would you do if God asked you to kill your own child? I imagine most of us would have been appalled by such a request, yet Abraham, so humble and trusting, took Isaac to Moriah, to do exactly what God asked of him. The writer of Hebrews stated in chapter 11 that Abraham believed God could raise up his son again.

In all honesty, none of us are certain how Abraham truly felt at the time. It's understandably difficult to wrap one's mind around that entire experience. The fact is, he made a decision to give what was most precious to him, to God. No complaints. No hesitation. In this season, God is looking for blind faith. He will ask some things of us, things that will twist us up inside. Things that will ruin some relationships we currently have. Yet, we must be ready to say yes!

Given that we are already in the great falling away, there are many among us in the church who will oppose what God has asked of you to do. Like the Pharisees did with Jesus, they will try to convince others that you are a devil, and not the messenger of God. Will you allow the hardened faces to stop you from doing God's will?

Write down where you struggle the most to do God's will. Expound on your biggest fears, then put them all before God in prayer. Only He can help us to overcome the fear of going against the grain.

A prayer: *Lord Jesus, help us to make the right decision to do Your will, no matter what it may cost us. Remind us that You are always here with us, even when the world is against us. We place our hearts into Your hands, in Jesus' name, Amen.*

Notes

Day 7 – Search Me, Oh God

Scripture: *[23]Search me, O God, and know my heart: try me, and know my thoughts: [24]And see if there be any wicked way in me, and lead me in the way everlasting.* Psalm 139: 23-24

Many years ago, at only twelve (12) years old, I was abused by a family friend. The experience itself had broken me more than I cared to admit to myself. I'd been traumatized. Months after the fact, I learned that a family member had been disseminating rumours about that same event contrary to how it actually happened. They'd even added more details and created other distasteful stories for their listeners to gobble up.

For a while, I was angry with that family member. Then I got saved and I told myself I was letting it go. More years passed, and then came a death in the family that brought that relative and I within the same space. The moment I laid eyes on that person, all the anger, the pain, the resentment returned like a train wreck.

It shocked me to my core! I'd been convinced that I'd dealt with it and was free, yet in that moment, I'd hated my relative. They had hurt me so badly, even caused others to have a warped mindset of me, and caused me unnecessary hurt on top of what I was already going through. I was struggling with unforgiveness.

Perhaps you're struggling with something in your heart as well. You want to move forward, but the hurt, the resentment, the unforgiveness is holding you back. Write down what hurts you. Ask the Lord to search you today and heal you where it hurts the most. In order to reset spiritually, we must let go of past hurts and live free in Christ Jesus.

A prayer: Father in heaven, *search us today. Show us where we've fallen short of Your righteousness, so that we may find our complete healing in You. Touch the hardened hearts, Lord, and help us to forgive as we are forgiven, in Jesus' holy name, Amen.*

Notes

Day 8 – Alive and…Well?

Scripture: [14]*But the Spirit of the Lord departed from Saul, and an evil spirit from the Lord troubled him.* 1 Samuel 16:14

In the latter part of 2022, my husband was asked to preach at a certain church. He'd preached there a couple of times before, so the atmosphere was quite familiar to us. On this particular Sunday, a young lady from the community had come in for prayer. Each time one of the ministers laid hands on her and began praying, she'd cough uncontrollably. When I got a chance to go to her after the service, I got wind of the issue. She was being choked from the inside by demons that had taken up residence inside her.

Today, there are more possessed people walking around than ever before. Satan has found his way into the souls of many out there, destroying them from the inside out. King Saul also struggled with an evil spirit. This evil spirit was sanctioned by God to torment Saul. Why? Because he disobeyed God and did what the people wanted instead. The king found himself in the belly of sin. It was clear from the start that Saul did not have a heart for the things of God. This gave room for an evil spirit to possess him the moment the Spirit of God left him.

Many of us are alive, breathing, but are we well? We may not be possessed by an evil spirit, but are we giving access to devils by disobeying God? And have we been making excuses for why we have to do things our way instead of His way? A spiritual reset requires that we close all access doors to the dark world, and give ourselves in complete submission to God. There is no life or wellness outside of that, despite what lying teachers and preachers say. Obedience to God is a must, not a maybe. It's time to choose your destiny. A living submissive or a walking dead!

A prayer: *Lord Jesus, we ask You to help us to be obedient and submissive to Your voice. Forgive us for failing to listen when You speak, and help us to do better, in Jesus' name, Amen.*

Notes

Day 9 – Cold, Hard Truths

Scripture: *²²Many will say to me in that day, Lord, Lord, have we not prophesied in thy name? and in thy name have cast out devils? and in thy name done many wonderful works? ²³And then will I profess unto them, I never knew you: depart from me, ye that work iniquity.* Matthew 7:22-23

Payday is possibly every working person's favourite time of the month. After those long, arduous hours of labour, we all want our reward. But what if at the end of the month, the figure in your bank account is way less than what you expected? Even worse, what if, upon enquiry, you found out that you wouldn't be getting a dime more because of your incompetence on the job? Whether that assessment is true or not, most of us would have been livid!

Jesus informed His disciples that not everyone who calls on His name will be rewarded with the pleasures of the Kingdom. The cold, hard truth in this telling is that many *Christians* out there doing the work will find themselves standing on the other side of the pearly gates. How is this even possible when you're busy working for the King? More importantly, how do we ensure that we never suffer this fate on that day when Jesus is ready to judge this world?

In verse 21 of Matthew 7, Jesus clearly identified those who would make it in His kingdom. It is those who do the will of His Father. What is the will of the Father, you ask? Simply listening to Jesus (Luke 9:35). There are some deep fundamental life principles that Jesus left with us that many of us have refused to follow over the years. We do the work, but we don't apply Jesus' teachings to our own lives. It is in the simple things that we fail. As we work for the Lord, let us remember to follow Jesus' life lessons. Our place in the kingdom depends on it.

A prayer: *Lord Jesus, help us to focus on the lessons You left behind for our learning so that we will know Your will and follow it while working for You, in Jesus' name, Amen.*

Notes

____

Day 10 – Selfish Desires

Scripture: *⁹And God said to Jonah, Doest thou well to be angry for the gourd? And he said, I do well to be angry, even unto death.* Jonah 4:9

When we were kids, my cousins and I used to play games together like most relatives do. There was one cousin in particular whom I was very close to. She was a sweet kid for the most part, but she had one fundamental flaw. She was ill-tempered. Whenever she lost in the games we played, she would fall into temper tantrums and would either destroy the game itself or start hitting others.

In the book of Jonah, we encounter a wicked nation that God was intent on destroying if they refused to change their ways. Jonah was supposed to preach to them so that they could turn, but he refused. After fighting a losing battle with God, he ended up doing the assignment, only to get angry with God when He turned His wrath away from the now repentant nation. Jonah's concern sat more with wanting his prophecy to come true than to see people be saved. As such, he went out of the city, sat and waited to see what would happen to Nineveh.

God confronted Jonah about His rotten behaviour. He created a tree to shade Jonah from the sun, then killed it shortly thereafter. This was a chance for Jonah to learn a lesson that people's lives were more important than his selfish desires, yet he was angry that God destroyed the tree and not the city. And isn't it so with some of us today? We are more concerned about our gifts than the people God gave us the gifts to serve. Selfishness is a grave hindrance to doing God's will. As we reset, let us strive to shake off our own evil desires and focus on what God desires most from us. Care for those who are lost. It's about Him, not us, always.

A prayer: *Lord, have mercy on us. Help us to become selfless, and to do Your will, not our own. Teach us to put others first, just like You put us first when You died for us, in Jesus' name, Amen.*

Notes

Day 11 – The Evil in Me

Scripture: *¹⁰But the chief priests consulted that they might put Lazarus also to death; ¹¹Because that by reason of him many of the Jews went away, and believed on Jesus.* John 12:10-11

One of the most staggering, yet sobering experiences I've had is watching a mighty man or woman of God stumble and fall. And I don't mean a physical fall. I'm talking about a horrid tumble into a life of sin that is sometimes even worse than the life they lived before Christ. "What were they thinking? No Christian should ever be caught doing such things!" That's usually our response. And it is true; it shouldn't happen, yet it does.

The opening scripture tells us of the Pharisees, and how they had consulted with each other about killing Lazarus. Poor Lazarus who'd already suffered and died, became a target for death again. And the threat came from none other than the religious leaders of the day! Why on earth would these men of God want this innocent man put to death?

It was simple. Evil ruled their hearts. Despite the holy garments they wore, envy toward Jesus consumed them, and because He was the one who raised Lazarus from the dead, Lazarus needed to die as well. This is what happens whenever we allow Satan to enter into partnership with our flesh. We may look at the Pharisees and shake our heads at their epic failure, but the truth is, any one of us could have fallen in the same belly of wickedness.

As we go through this process of reset, let us each search our hearts and confront the evil in us, no matter how small it seems, and uproot it by the power of the Holy Ghost. A clean heart and a pure mind are what God require of us. Let's pursue it!

A prayer: *Lord Jesus, help us to have a clean heart and a pure mind before You. Give us the will to overcome the evil seed of our flesh, so we may never be ruled by it. Grant us divine strength and favour in this season of change, in Jesus' name, Amen.*

Notes

Day 12 – The Victim Game

Scripture: *⁸That all of you have conspired against me, and there is none that sheweth me that my son hath made a league with the son of Jesse, and there is none of you that is sorry for me, or sheweth unto me that my son hath stirred up my servant against me, to lie in wait, as at this day?* 1 Samuel 22:8

We live in an era where being a victim means you're a hero. Everyone has a story, and we are all competing to see who can tell the worst one yet, for it means more likes and more views for us on social media. The downside to this is that it makes those who are true victims of terrible circumstances get drowned out in the noise.

King Saul was a man who loved to play the victim game as well. After being rejected by God for His disobedience, he constantly wanted everyone around him to pity him. In the verse mentioned above, he told his servants that they had all conspired against him, simply because they hadn't told him David was in town. Young David had been anointed king in his stead, and Saul was intent on killing him before that could ever happen. He expected all of Israel to be on board with this wicked thing, no questions asked. But even his own heir, Jonathan, protected David from him. The real victim in the story was David, who was forced out of his own home and country by a selfish king, and was on the run for his life.

Only self-serving, narcissistic people blame others for the things they did. In this period of reset, let us be sure to not play the blame game whenever we are in the wrong. It's a trait of our sinful nature to put the blame on someone else, but if we only place our hearts before God, He will change us and make us new from the inside out. The truth is, even narcissists can be saved!

A prayer: *Lord, touch my heart, cleanse me and save me from my sinful nature. Help me to not play the victim card when I'm in the wrong, but seek forgiveness instead, in Jesus' name, Amen.*

Notes

Day 13 – Give Me Smooth Sayings!

Scripture: *⁹That this is a rebellious people, lying children, children that will not hear the law of the Lord: ¹⁰Which say to the seers, See not; and to the prophets, Prophesy not unto us right things, speak unto us smooth things, prophesy deceits:* Isaiah 30:9-10

We all can agree there are no better sermons to our ears than the ones that promise us prosperity and ultimate success in life. They get us pumped, excited, make us feel good about ourselves, even when we haven't done anything worthwhile that could propel us into these fantastical blessings the preacher is trying to convince us we will receive.

On the other hand, we don't do well with those loud-mouthed prophets who come to rebuke us and set us straight. I couldn't begin to count the many times I've witnessed prophets and prophetesses being silenced and led outside the church building to be calmed down and shamed for disrupting the service. Just like in Isaiah's days, the church struggles to listen to truth. We have those itching ears that prefer to hear sweet-nothings from Satan, instead of reproof from our Bridegroom, Jesus Christ. Lies are like milk and cookies to us. Truth is like a bowl of green salad. Without the dressing, of course.

To accept God's will, we must grow tougher skin and be ready to hear from the Lord where we've fallen short. Where we've strayed from His presence. Where we've set our own lives on the fires of hell. We must be prepared to trim off the excess weight that is holding us back, and be completely surrendered to God's will and purpose for our lives. Smooth sayings are for those who don't want change. Do you desire change in your life?

A prayer: *Lord Jesus, we are bombarded on every side with smooth, lying words meant to keep us happy, yet bound. Help us to listen to Your voice even when it's hard, so that we may grow in You, Amen.*

Notes

Day 14 – Still Sitting on The Fence

Scripture: *²¹And Elijah came unto all the people, and said, How long halt ye between two opinions? if the Lord be God, follow him: but if Baal, then follow him. And the people answered him not a word.* 1 Kings 18:21

When I was ten years old, the Lord impressed upon my heart to give my life to Him. I didn't understand much about living a Christian life at the time, even though I'd been reared in church. Hence, in my teen years, it became difficult to live a clean life before God. Like every other teenager around me, I was curious to try new things, though I promised myself I wouldn't go too far.

Other Christian teens I knew, and even some of the adults, also wanted to sit on the fence instead of going all in with God. Girls who were virgins made sure their boyfriends did everything but break their hymen. Boys would masturbate to calm their unruly hormones. It seemed like a win-win situation at the time. This was exactly where Israel found itself under the rule of Ahab and Jezebel. With wicked monarchs on the throne, Israel sat on the fence about who they wanted to give their worship. This is what the scripture calls lukewarmness.

God hates lukewarmness. In the book of Revelation, He warned the Laodicean church about this very state. He threatened to spit them out if they didn't change their behaviour (Rev. 3:14-19). Indeed, no one can serve two masters (Matt. 6:24). Therefore, in this season of reset, we must make up our minds to give God all or nothing. Towing the fence and hoping for the best will not work. God proved His loyalty to us by giving His only Begotten Son to die for us. It's time we proved our loyalty to Him by being completely sold out to Him!

A prayer: *Lord, we have failed to give You our all. Forgive us and help us to choose the good over the evil, withholding nothing. In Jesus' name, Amen.*

Notes

Day 15 - I AM THAT I AM

Scripture: [14]*And God said unto Moses, I Am That I Am: and he said, Thus shalt thou say unto the children of Israel, I Am hath sent me unto you.* Exodus 3:14

I was scrolling through social media one day when I came across a certain post. Though I can't remember the details of the post itself, I specifically recall a comment that was made, discrediting the post, claiming that there were many other "gods" in existence before Jesus Christ was even born. This person clearly thought that this meant the Christian God was not the one true God, but one of many gods out there.

What the commentator did not realize is that God did not come into existence at some blip in time. The birth of Jesus Christ did not mean another god had finally come into existence. In the book of Exodus when Moses came face to face with God, the Lord told him, "I AM THAT I AM."

God is. He always was and always will be God, even when mankind comes up with other gods to worship. The birth of Jesus Christ was the self-existing eternal God preparing a body in time to die for our sins. This is why Jesus told the Pharisees in John 8:58, "Before Abraham was, I AM." It was the eternal God speaking through Him.

As we reconnect with God, let us be mindful of His greatness and power. He is not merely another god in a long line of gods interfering in the affairs of men. He is the one true God, Maker of heaven and earth. Take some time today to think of Him, and appreciate Him just for who He is. Our God is amazing!

A prayer: *Lord Jesus, we acknowledge You today as the great God and King of heaven and earth. All things created are Yours. None else stands beside You, none else can take Your place. Be exalted Lord forever and ever, in Jesus' name, Amen.*

Notes

Day 16 - Elevated Mindset

Scripture: *⁵Let this mind be in you, which was also in Christ Jesus:* Philippians 2:5

The mind is that part of us that controls our thoughts, imaginations and emotions. It is the gateway of our souls, which is the battleground of good and evil. The things we do and say on a daily basis are a result of what is happening in our minds. Proverbs 23:7 states, "For as he thinketh in his heart, so is he: Eat and drink, saith he to thee; but his heart is not with thee."

In the passage of Philippians 2, we are exhorted to have a mindset akin to Jesus Christ's. What kind of mind did Jesus have? According to the writer, Jesus Christ found Himself in the form of a man, and although He was the God of glory, He humbled Himself and became obedient unto the death of the cross. As human beings, we love to show the world who we are and what we've accomplished in life. This is why millions of posts are made every day on social media about some new achievement or how-to videos from so-called *experts.*

While there is nothing wrong with sharing our successes or expertise with others, we must be careful to not get caught up in the world's ideologies and practices. Not everything is meant to be shared. Sometimes it is better to take the lower seat, even when you are the most powerful one standing in the room. Jesus was the most powerful man walking around in His day, yet not many caught on to it until it was too late, like the centurion in Matthew 27:54. Let us be mindful to live in that place of humility, serving others and practising putting others' needs before our own. It's exactly what Jesus did when He walked this earth and we must strive to be like Him.

A prayer: *Lord Jesus, thank You for all that You have blessed us with. Give us an elevated mindset that transcends selfishness and focuses on the needs of others. We want the essence of our being to reflect You and only You, in Jesus' name, Amen.*

Notes

Day 17 - The Fiery Darts of The Wicked

Scripture: *[16]Above all, taking the shield of faith, wherewith ye shall be able to quench all the fiery darts of the wicked.* Ephesians 6:16

Back in July of 2023, my husband and I celebrated our birthdays together. It was one of the best we'd had and we couldn't be more grateful for those deliciously happy moments. However, it was only days later that we went to the doctor and received some awful news that shook us both to our very core. After the high of our birthdays, we were knocked off balance by our situation!

By now, you're probably facing the fiery darts of the wicked while soldiering through this reset. If it hasn't yet, it will commence soon. When you least expect it, Satan tosses one of his most lethal weapons your way, sending you flying a hundred feet in the air before landing flat on your back. It's a rather painful experience, filled with feelings of hopelessness that you may not be able to get back up. To fight.

His blow is radical, but the damage you see is only an illusion. In your hand, you're holding something much more powerful than any dart the enemy could throw at you. The shield of faith! Faith is a weapon that when wielded, staggers the enemy and brings his plans to nought. Our faith in God destroys yokes. Our faith in God breaks fetters. Our faith in God brings healing! Our faith in God discombobulates the work of Satan and scatters his forces!

Now get up, warrior. Grip your shield and fight like You have a God to defend You. Because you do! The devil played dirty, and now seems to be winning, but God has the final word on the matter. They say it's never over until the fat lady sings? Well, it isn't over until God says it is!

A prayer: *Lord Jesus, our shields of faith are lifted today. Defend us, Oh God, and give us complete victory, in Jesus' name, Amen.*

Notes

Day 18 - On Shaky Foundation

Scripture: *³If the foundations be destroyed, what can the righteous do?* Psalm 11:3

Foundation is the base upon which structures are built. Every building we see around us has some kind of foundation that keeps it from toppling over. Without a proper foundation, everything around us would collapse with the wind.

Similarly, our relationship with God needs a firm foundation on which to stand. As the writer said in the scripture above, what can we do if the base of our belief system is destroyed? This is the time to examine the groundwork of our belief system. Why are you a Christian? What were you expecting when you entered into a relationship with Jesus? What are your expectations now?

The right foundation requires that our belief system be without fault. We must believe in the death, burial and resurrection of the Lord Jesus Christ to be saved. We must repent of our sins, put on His name in water baptism and receive His Holy Spirit (Acts 2:38). We must have a clear understanding that Jesus Christ is our righteousness (2Cor 5:21), and nothing we do by our own power can earn us a place at His side. Without this foundation of righteousness, we are merely wasting our time.

It's time to check our foundation. Righteousness is what God requires of us, and we can only achieve this through the Lord Jesus' work on the cross. Otherwise, we are plagued by our wicked hearts, awaiting the judgement of God, and that is shaky foundation. It's time to build on the solid rock, where we are sure to find peace, stability, and security that can withstand every wind of doctrine that is not from the throne room of God.

A prayer: *Lord, help us to realize that our righteousness is filth before You, but the righteousness we obtain through Jesus Christ is our salvation and solid foundation. Help us to hold fast to this firm foundation, in Jesus' name, Amen.*

Notes

Day 19 - Shady Prayers

Scripture: *³Ye ask, and receive not, because ye ask amiss, that ye may consume it upon your lusts.* James 4:3

On Day 13, we dove into prosperity messages and how much we love to hear them. Of course, there's nothing like a good message about blessings galore in our future and how God will cause us to rejoice over our enemies. Add a dash of Psalm 23:5 as reference, and we are ready to run the aisle in victory. Prospering over our enemies gives us a dopamine hit like no other!

Not only do we enjoy hearing it; we also love to pray for prosperity more than anything else. Though many of us have never moved to do anything that would equate to the kind of riches we would like to garner in our lives, we insist on decreeing and declaring blessings untold.

Why? Why do we pray for riches untold? Is it that we desire to build the kingdom of God with our God-given wealth? Or do we just want it to heap it upon our own lusts? To be clear, nothing is wrong with having wealth as a child of God. Abraham, Job, David and many of our forefathers were wealthy men. The difference between those men and many of us today is that they didn't pray for riches for the pleasure of it or to make their enemies burn with jealousy. Nothing was "shady" or deceitful about their prayers to God. All they wanted was to please God.

As we talk to the Lord about our desires today, let us explore the root of those requests. The Lord requires good motives behind every prayer we pray, or else He will not hear us! At the end of the day, it's never really about us, but about God being glorified through us.

A prayer: *Lord Jesus, our motives are sometimes not pure. Forgive us and help us to develop good motives for every prayer we pray, so that You may be glorified in us, in Jesus' name, Amen.*

Notes

Day 20 - The Murmuring Christian

Scripture: *¹⁰Neither murmur ye, as some of them also murmured, and were destroyed of the destroyer.* 1 Corinthians 10:10

My late grandmother used to tell me stories of times in her younger life when things were tough. Sometimes, there wasn't enough in the cupboards to eat, which meant each child would get less than usual. The children would form a line and my grandfather would give each of the kids at least two crackers to have with their tea. And there was always someone murmuring about how little the food was. Whenever this happened, my grandfather would simply move on to the next child and hand him/her what the murmuring child was supposed to receive.

In this modern age where gentle parenting is the norm, many would argue that this was child abuse. After all, a child or two was going to go to bed without food, simply because they asked for more. Still, it was one of those lessons that taught them to be content with what they had until God blessed them with more. As Christians, we oftentimes find ourselves murmuring and complaining about how difficult life is, and how God has failed to provide what we need, not realizing that all that time, we were blessed beyond measure.

The children of Israel did the same. No matter how many miracles God performed on their behalf, they constantly murmured against Him and His faithful servant, Moses. In the end, it caused them to miss out on the promised land! Today, they are used as an example to the church, for our learning (Hebrews 3:7-19). Let us not be caught in the same sin of ungratefulness. Trust in God! We've proven Him too many times to murmur our way into the sin of unbelief! It's time to stop complaining and start praising the Lord for all the blessings He has given us!

A prayer: *Heavenly Father, forgive us for murmuring against You. Help us to rejoice even in the bad times, knowing You will always come through for us. In Jesus' name, Amen.*

Notes

Day 21 – The Wrong Enemy

Scripture: [12]*For we wrestle not against flesh and blood, but against principalities, against powers, against the rulers of the darkness of this world, against spiritual wickedness in high places.* Ephesians 6:12

When I was a child, I was not good at physical altercations. To be precise, I was one of those children who did their best to be seen but not heard. Yet, in some twisted way, this often made me the victim of bullying at school. As I write this devotion, I can vividly recall a couple of those moments when I would get beat up by kids who thought I was the perfect punching bag, given my quiet demeanour. I never really fought back, not until around high school. That was when I managed to hurt two boys on separate occasions out of boiling anger.

Fighting is our way of defending ourselves against a perceived enemy. Be it physical or emotional, we oftentimes come in contact with that one person who just rubs us the wrong way. The human reaction is to see the person in front of you as the enemy, but Paul reminds us in Ephesians 6 that our real enemy is not that family member, that co-worker, or that church brother or sister you just can't bond with no matter how hard you try.

Satan secretly pits people against each other every single day. This is why wars happen. This is why blood siblings end up murdering each other. No one sees the invisible puppeteer pulling the strings of our cognized enemy. As you toil through this reset, consider that person in your life whom you deem your enemy. Instead of resisting them at every turn, start praying for them and doing good to them as Jesus exhorted us in Matthew 5:44. The change may not happen with them, but it certainly will in you.

A prayer: *Heavenly Father, Satan wants to keep us fighting among ourselves, but today we pray that our eyes will be opened to the true enemy of our souls, in Jesus' name, Amen.*

Notes

Day 22 – The Wrong Friend

Scripture: *³But Amnon had a friend, whose name was Jonadab, the son of Shimeah David's brother: and Jonadab was a very subtil man.* 2 Samuel 13:3

Back in high school, I met a girl who instantly became one of my closest friends. She was such a sweetheart, I couldn't help wanting to be around her all the time. However, somewhere in the middle of our friendship, I found out she was dating an older man. As time went by, she started to give me advice about men. She wanted me and another close friend to spend a weekend together with her boyfriend and other men, where we would engage in intercourse with these strangers for the fun of it. To date, it was one of the worst advice I'd ever received from a friend.

Amnon, David's prodigy of a son, had a friend who gave him terrible advice as well. The young man was obsessed with his half-sister, Tamar, and could think of nothing else but having her. If Jonadab, his best friend and cousin, had been a good friend, he would have steered him away from wickedness. But the scriptures rightfully called him a subtle man, for so he was. Because of his not-so-friendly advice, an innocent girl was raped and then tossed aside like yesterday's garbage. Amnon later lost his life at the hands of Tamar's full-brother, Absalom. Such a painful chain of events, and all because the prince listened to the wrong friend.

Take this time to assess your friends. Who are you taking advice from? Is the advice you are receiving to your benefit, or your demise? Not everyone who draws close to you is a true friend. Some are simply there because they get to benefit from you. It's time to dig through your friends list and assess your inner circle. It's going to be painful, but worth it in the end.

A prayer: *Lord, help us to discern and choose our inner circle of friends with godly wisdom, in Jesus' name, Amen.*

Notes

Day 23 - The Lust of The Flesh

Scripture: [1]*There is therefore now no condemnation to them which are in Christ Jesus, who walk not after the flesh, but after the Spirit.* Romans 8:1

Sin is a hereditary disease passed down from generation to generation since the time of Adam until now. It affects every one of us in various ways, depending on our nature, how we were nurtured as well as life experiences. Every sin we commit stems from a fleshly desire doing its best to overpower that God-conscious part of us. Though we have the power to choose, history has proven time and again that mankind prefers to feed the raging monster within than to yield himself to Almighty God. As such, we are left grappling through a world filled with self-gratification.

Lust is a strong, wicked desire. To be ruled by it is to be completely out of control of the self, with little rationality behind our actions. On Day 22, we talked about Amnon and how he treated his sister, Tamar. It was lust that consumed him and turned him into something even he himself could not recognize. A demon-like character who comes to kill, steal and destroy.

Are you struggling with lust? Do you feel yourself burning with that intense emotion when that one person is somewhere nearby? Are you imagining thoughts of being with someone else's spouse? Perhaps you are lusting after someone's house, or car, or job. Either way, it's time to fix this issue. To serve God freely, we must address every root of wickedness within us. Put them before God with a sincere heart and watch Him do a mighty work in you. The man who makes Jesus Christ the centre of his world is the man who resists the evil and chooses the good. Make a covenant with your eyes (Job 31:1). It's time to put this unruly flesh under subjection.

A prayer: Heavenly *Father, help us to resist the wicked desires of our flesh and choose You always, in Jesus' name, Amen.*

Notes

Day 24 - The Lust of The Eyes

Scripture: *[20]Hell and destruction are never full; so the eyes of man are never satisfied.* Proverbs 27:20

A friend of mine lost an uncle some years ago through violence. When my husband and I inquired to find out what happened, we were shocked to learn that it was his own employees who had robbed him and murdered him in cold blood. He'd paid them all their due hire, with bonuses, but some were still not happy about what they were getting. They wanted more. It was Christmas time after all and they wanted to have as much as the boss did.

This is the kind of world we live in today. Everybody wants more, even when they didn't work for it. Most of us can probably think of that one family member or friend who will get angry with you if they don't get what they want from you, even if you came through for them 99% of the time. Some people will just never be satisfied, no matter how much you've already given them.

Have you found yourself craving material things? Do you consider compromising at times to get ahead in the game? Are you finding it difficult to be content with what the Lord has blessed you with so far? Nothing is wrong with desiring things, but if that desire causes us to step out of God's cloak of righteousness to get what we want, then it has turned into lust of the eyes and we are just about on our way to hell and destruction.

Like Jesus did when the devil took him on the mountain to show him all the kingdoms of the world, rebuke the enemy and his devices! Let him know you will never bow to him, but will put your trust wholly in the Lord.

A prayer: *Lord Jesus, help us to walk the path You chose. To be completely subjected to the Father's will. Help us to resist the world and choose righteousness. In Jesus' name, Amen.*

Notes

Day 25 - The Pride of Life

Scripture: [12]*Before destruction the heart of man is haughty, and before honour is humility.* Proverbs 18:12

In the ninth grade, we had a classmate who was excellent at Math. He could understand the most complicated questions and was even better at explaining them to us than our teacher ever could. This made him cocky. Though he'd decided to help the rest of us who weren't as good as him, he was like a peacock walking around with feathers prettier than the other birds around him. Shockingly, when we did our exams sometime after that, all the people he'd helped got A's and B's while his grade was bordering on a D. It knocked the wind out of us all, but more so, it had humiliated our math genius.

Pride is the sin that will cause a man to go to the car mart and buy the most expensive car on loan, just to make himself look good to his friends and acquaintances. It is the sin that makes women wear excessive makeup to enhance their beauty. It's also what causes people to enter into ungodly deals for the sake of image. The prideful soul will even go as far as destroying others to make themselves look good. This is why God resists the proud (James 4:6).

Have you entered into some shady schemes for the sake of imagery? Did you embarrass someone lately just to make yourself look like the better person? Pride is the sin that causes God to back away from us. No matter how much we clap, sing or speak in tongues, He will never accept a proud and wicked heart. But as the scripture says, "...a broken and a contrite heart, O God, thou wilt not despise." Psalm 51:17. Let's work to get rid of the little things that hinder us in our relationship with Christ. There is nothing more beautiful to the Lord than a meek, submissive soul, fit for the Master's use.

A prayer: *Holy Father, help us to have a heart of humility before You, not postured toward wickedness, but learning to be more like You. In Jesus' name, Amen.*

Notes

Day 26 – Candid Shots

Scripture: *⁸This people draweth nigh unto me with their mouth, and honoureth me with their lips; but their heart is far from me. ⁹But in vain they do worship me, teaching for doctrines the commandments of men.* Matthew 15:8-9

Candid shots can be the best or worst of you. I'd been caught in a few myself over the years, mostly by my playful husband, and some of them have caused me to chase him around our home to get those pictures deleted as soon as possible! Others come out so beautiful, it makes you wonder where that side of you was all that time.

In the presence of those we respect, we tend to want to put out the best version of ourselves, even when we know deep down that the image we are portraying is a lie. Israel, for centuries, operated like this with God. Jehovah didn't just want their words. He also wanted their hearts. However, the people of Israel were oftentimes busy thinking of their own business or lusting after other gods. They preferred man-made doctrines over God's teachings. This is why Isaiah made the prophecy that Jesus, in the gospels, so fittingly quoted in His day.

We, today, are not much different from ancient Israel. Many times, we pray out of ritual and not necessarily because we want to have a genuine conversation with Jesus. We use all the buzzwords that are supposed to make God feel good, yet our minds are barely on Him. We'd rather think about the bills or gas for the car. Imagine talking to a friend, only to realize a couple of minutes in that they were distracted and not listening the entire time. If you're anything like me, you'd probably go silent for the rest of the day. This is how God feels when we meet with Him out of duty and not desire. His desire is to have our hearts just like we have His. Love should not be a one-way street.

A prayer: *Lord, forgive us for our failure to worship You from the heart. We give ourselves to You completely, in Jesus' name, Amen.*

Notes

Day 27 – Hello Joy, Nice to Meet You!

Scripture: *[11]These things have I spoken unto you, that my joy might remain in you, and that your joy might be full.* John 15:11

Many of us have worked for years trying to find happiness in our jobs, education, hobbies, marriages and even children. For the most part, we do find that spark of cheerfulness, yet it tends to be fleeting, forever urging us to gain more and more to satisfy that agonizing need. In the end, what we'll find is that there is always something else missing in our lives no matter how hard we try to fill the void. Every human being on the face of the earth has experienced that note of wistfulness, mourning something that felt only just within our reach, yet dreadfully unattainable on our own.

Part of this reset is about finding that inner peace we all long for. Peace that brings us overwhelming joy amid our most dire circumstances. Jesus' disciples were at that place; they needed joy in its fullness. It was in chapter 14 of John that Jesus started His goodbye speech, and it made them sorrowful. They didn't want their Master to leave. But Jesus had some good news for them. Through this tragic loss they were about to experience, they would gain so much more. Certainly, it didn't feel that way in the moment, but through the promised Comforter, these same disciples would soon learn the power of unspeakable joy.

True, unending joy comes from the Holy Ghost. We may experience happiness from time to time, yet it hardly compares to the joy that comes from the Lord. It's time to embrace that joy! Despite the pain and struggles you're facing, there is an inexplicable bliss that comes with knowing God is for you! If you have not yet received the Holy Ghost, it is time. Experience the joy of the Lord today!

A prayer: *Lord Jesus, thank You for the joy of the Holy Ghost. Even when the storms are raging around us, our joy is full. We bless Your name, Lord, in Jesus' name, Amen.*

Notes

Day 28 – Steadfast Service

Scripture: [58]*Therefore, my beloved brethren, be ye stedfast, unmoveable, always abounding in the work of the Lord, forasmuch as ye know that your labour is not in vain in the Lord.* 1 Corinthians 15:58

Any seasoned Christian understands that our walk with God is no straight path without obstacles. The road is narrow, long, winding, and filled with thorns and thistles. When the trials of life hit us hard, the strongest among us are able to stand flatfooted in Christ, comes what may. The rest of us tend to either stagger out of place or fall flat on our face. That shift, whatever form it takes, has the ability to knock us completely out of the race.

The Corinthian church was being plagued by naysayers who wanted to convince the people of God that there was no resurrection of the dead. Such an audacious statement for any Christian to make, considering our entire faith leans on the basis of Jesus Christ's resurrection from the dead.

Paul rightfully spoke out, ripping apart the seed of deceit that was being planted in the hearts of the people to overthrow their faith in the risen Lamb of God. His encouragement to his hearers was simply this. Remain steadfast in your faith. Don't let anyone trick you into believing a lie.

Are there liars lurking around, trying to destroy your faith? Trying to discredit that wonderful joy you've found in Christ? Teaching wicked doctrines of devils to throw you off course? It's time to double down on the truth of God's word. The enemy seeks to destroy your steadfastness in God but be encouraged today. Your work in the Lord will never be in vain.

A prayer: *Father, thank You for opening my eyes to truth. Help me to stand steadfast in my faith and service to You, despite the naysayers. In Jesus' holy name, Amen.*

Notes

Day 29 – God's Word, Settled

Scripture: [89]*For ever, O Lord, thy word is settled in heaven.*
Psalm 119:89

In recent times, perhaps the last two decades or so, we have been experiencing a radical shift in the ideologies of the world, an atrocity which undoubtedly began in the spirit realm. Things that used to be normal, like heterosexual marriages or male/female gender identity, are now being treated as obsolete. The word of God is no longer revered as the authority that rules our society. And so today, we find people openly declaring that the Bible is a lie and that we were being kept under bondage all these years.

In the churches, we also find Christians who are willing to meet the world halfway by twisting God's word just a bit to include the sinner who refuses to be anything but the wrongdoer he/she is. What was once truth now becomes a heinous lie to be done away with for fear that it will hurt the feelings of those who contend with our doctrine.

As you go through this reset, bear in mind that God does not bow Himself to the whims of anyone. He is holy, righteous and perfect in all His ways. It is us who are in dire need of Him, not the other way around. As the world changes for the worse with each passing day, we must remember that we were never intended to be friends with it. We are a transformed people who await the coming of our Lord and Saviour, Jesus Christ. Our purpose is not to change God's word to suit the wicked. It is to show men that they are lost sheep in need of their Shepherd. God's word is settled in heaven. There is nothing you or I can do to change it. Lies will always be lies and truth will always be truth. It is time to assess, see where we've changed God's word to glorify sin and repent.

A prayer: *Lord Jesus, we, as Your body, are failing to stand for truth. Help us to stand and defend Your word instead of fighting against it. In Jesus' holy name, Amen.*

Notes

Day 30 – Not the Submissive Type?

Scripture: *²And they said, Hath the Lord indeed spoken only by Moses? hath he not spoken also by us? And the Lord heard it.* Numbers 12:2

A certain woman at a particular church that I used to attend, was a menace to the pastor of the assembly. At least, that was how he felt about her. She was one of those people who seemed inclined to do the opposite of what her spiritual leader said, even if it was good, solid advice. She struggled with a spirit of rebellion and thus became the bane of this pastor's existence. She might have shaved off a decade of his life as well.

The truth is, she isn't the only Christian in the world who struggles with submission. Many *saints* are quicker to submit to their bosses than their pastors. Additionally, many Christian women go out of their way to not submit to their husbands as well. We are in an era where the very idea of submission is revolting. Every day we see on social media that people have become more and more disrespectful to those God put as heads of the churches.

It's not a new phenomenon, however. In Moses' day, his brother and sister spoke against him and the Lord heard it. God spat in Miriam's face and turned her into a leper. It was Moses who had to pray to the Lord for her deliverance. The same man of God whom they criticized and stirred up a rebellion against.

Let's take this as a lesson to not speak cruelly against the ones God set in place to lead the churches. If you struggle with a non-submissive spirit, it is time to put it before the Lord. There is nothing too hard for Him to fix. Never forget that in God's eyes, rebellion is like witchcraft and disobedience as iniquity and idolatry (1Samuel 15:23).

A prayer: *Father, we have sinned against You and Your word. Give us a heart of submission, so we can grow and be fruitful in Your kingdom, in Jesus' name, Amen.*

Notes

Day 31 – Breaking Ungodly Habits

Scripture: *⁹And now also the axe is laid unto the root of the trees: every tree therefore which bringeth not forth good fruit is hewn down, and cast into the fire.* Luke 3:9

Those of us who have been in church long enough have seen the good, the bad, the ugly. Unlike the new converts, we understand that church life is not a bed of roses. It's more like a psych ward trying to handle the different cases that come to it week after week. People need Jesus, and we are the channel through which healing and deliverance come. Of course, it's going to be a hot mess every now and then!

One of the most shocking things, however, is bumping into Christians who've been in church for decades, doing things they know is unlawful for any child of God to do. They don't steal, or sleep around or use profane language, but they take away people's justice. They take credit for things they know they didn't do. They shut up their bowels of compassion when a brethren needs their help.

John the Baptist in Luke chapter 3, had some of those religious people to deal with in his day. He made them realize that just because they were Abraham's children didn't mean they were righteous. Likewise, I would say, just because we have been baptized in the name of Jesus Christ and filled with the Holy Ghost, means that we cannot be in danger of hell fire. We may not be committing *the big sins*, but the little ones are just as dangerous and may cause us to lose out on our salvation.

So you've never drank or smoked in your life. That's good. But have you ever mistreated the poor? Did you slander your brother/sister's name just because you don't like them? Let's take the time to confront ourselves and dig up the little things in us that God is not pleased with.

Let's pray: *Lord Jesus, help me to see every wicked way in me, no matter how small it seems, and repent, in Jesus' name, Amen.*

Notes

Day 32 - My Tongue, My Enemy

Scripture: *⁶And the tongue is a fire, a world of iniquity: so is the tongue among our members, that it defileth the whole body, and setteth on fire the course of nature; and it is set on fire of hell.* James 3:6

As I looked up the text for today's devotional, I was brought back to two relatives of mine who've always had a problem with their tongues. Whenever those tongues started wagging, I would immediately go on high alert. To this day, everything they say is always taken with a grain of salt, since more times than not, the story has been edited with dramatic flair for the purpose of entertaining the listeners while humiliating the subjects in question.

The Bible describes the tongue as a fire. And what a perfect portrayal, seeing this little body part can destroy as many lives as fire can and in as little time as well! Proverbs 15:23 tells us that a word spoken in due season is good. But imagine a word spoken at just the wrong time and in the worst of situations? It has the opposite effect, of course. Sadly, many Christians today struggle to control their tongue. They find insurmountable pleasure in talking about their brothers and sisters in a way unbecoming of their station, and by it do more harm than good in the house of God.

Are you a talebearer? Has your tongue been used as a weapon in Satan's hand to destroy relationships? It's time for a repentance session. God is open and ready to forgive if you will only yield yourself to Him. No matter how long you've been in the church, it's never too late to place your faults before God. Salvation is a process, a journey, an adventure. So, take the leap. Allow the Spirit to move upon your tongue today and use it as a force of righteousness in the earth.

Let's pray: *Lord Jesus, some days, my tongue is my worst enemy. Help me to get it under control, so that I may speak only with righteousness and justice, in Jesus' name, Amen.*

Notes

Day 33 – All Churched Out

Scripture: *⁶Behold, thou desirest truth in the inward parts: and in the hidden part thou shalt make me to know wisdom.* Psalm 51:6

In the famous song, sung by the talented Tamela Mann, "Take Me to the King," one specific line always stood out to me. "I'm all churched out," the tune says. To me, being "all churched out," means I'm exhausted, overwhelmed, drained of all my energy and intolerant of the current routine of church life.

Many of us have found ourselves in that place at some point in our Christian journey. In these turbulent moments, we find it difficult to pray, to fast, to read the word, or even to attend church services. It's almost like being extremely hungry, but having no idea what to eat because everything available to us has become unpalatable. It's a kind of misery that doesn't budge easily, no matter how hard to try.

In moments like these, God desires for us to be open and true with Him. We tend to say a lot of things to God that we don't mean, simply because they are the *right* things to say. If you're feeling frustrated in your walk with God, it's time to have a heart-to-heart with the King. Once we get to that place where we start being completely honest with Him, we will open the door to learn heavenly wisdom straight from His throne room.

The Lord truly hears us when we pray. Surely, my earthly father can take only so much from my sisters and me! But with God, He'll open you up to greater spiritual things that will transform you in ways you never would have imagined. Usually, when change is needed, it is those who feel the burden that are being called to begin the process. Lay your cares on Jesus today and watch Him use you for His glory!

Let's pray: *Heavenly Father, I am tired of the routine of church life. I need more from You. Grant me heavenly wisdom. Help me to see You in all Your wonderful glory, in Jesus' name, Amen.*

Notes

Day 34 - Turning Point

Scripture: *⁵I have heard of thee by the hearing of the ear: but now mine eye seeth thee. ⁶Wherefore I abhor myself, and repent in dust and ashes.* Job 42:5-6

A turning point can be described as a moment of profound change, a decisive shift that alters the trajectory of our life's chronicle. It's the junction where our choices, circumstances, and emotions converge, leading us towards a new course or perspective. These moments can arise from various experiences, such as in the case of Brother Job, who was taken through a series of frightful, fiery trials, meant, on the part of Satan, to destroy him.

On Day 33, we discussed being all churched out in our walk with God. Once we become authentic in our communication with the Lord, He will take us to places only He, as God, can. Like Job, you are certain to reach that well-needed turning point that will mature you spiritually, giving you a fresh, new vision, not only about the Lord, but also about the self. The turning point brings growth, transformation and clarity. Your view on just about everything changes as you reevaluate your priorities and embrace change as the Lord leads. Nothing will look the same to you ever again.

To achieve this kind of spiritual growth, you must be completely sold out to God's wisdom. That means you will have to let go of what you think you know and be committed to adhering to God's modus operandi, even if your very nature goes against it. That's a solid turning point in any Christian's life. This is where God begins to "show us great and mighty things that we did not know" (Jeremiah 33:3). Indeed, there are many things that the Lord Jesus wants to share with us. Are you ready?

Let's pray: *I've seen you in all Your glory, Lord. Now I pray that my heart will become one with Yours, and Your ways will become my ways, in Jesus' name, Amen.*

Notes

Day 35 - Back to My First Love

Scripture: *⁴Nevertheless I have somewhat against thee, because thou hast left thy first love.* Revelation 2:4

Having been married to the love of my life for the past decade, there are a few things that I've discovered about marriage. One is that you can be so caught up in the day-to-day activities in your life that you miss out on what's most important. Like love. When Chris and I first met, our love was like a thousand fiery stars shooting across the sky all at once. After a decade together, those stars are still travelling, just not firing as maniacally as they were before. We've settled into a routine of comfort, oftentimes forgetting the crazy things we used to do together that would spice up our relationship.

Likewise, we sometimes fall into such a comfortable routine in our relationship with God that we fail to keep the stars firing from one end of heaven to the next. The Lord Jesus is zealous toward us. He doesn't enjoy lukewarm love. All the things we do to build His kingdom on Earth are good. Still, we must be cognizant of the fact that love is what He requires the most from us. In John 14:23, Jesus rightly points out that those who love Him, do what He says. Is there anything God wants more than obedient children?

While we perfect our works on earth, let's not forget our first love. The reason we, the church, entered into this covenant with Him in the first place is because we fell in love with Him who loved us first. When you love someone, you do almost anything to make that person happy, right? Christ is coming back for an obedient, submissive Bride who is madly in love with Him and can't wait to spend eternity with Him. It's time to rediscover that passionate love for the Lord!

Let's pray: *Lord Jesus, we've been so distracted from our relationship with You. Help us to rediscover and explore that deep, insatiable love for You, in Jesus' name, Amen.*

Notes

Day 36 - The Disciple Whom Jesus Loves

Scripture: [21]*He that hath my commandments, and keepeth them, he it is that loveth me: and he that loveth me shall be loved of my Father, and I will love him, and will manifest myself to him.* John 14:21

If you're like me, you probably frowned in confusion the very first time you read Romans 9:13. It quotes from Malachi 1:2-3, in which God declares that He loves Jacob but hates Esau. Inconceivable! How could God hate anyone? He is the epitome of love. He should not be hating anyone!

Those who have read the story of the twin boys in its entirety, however, know the meaning and motive behind the Lord's words. Esau was a disobedient son who married strange women against his parents' will. He also disregarded his birthright just because he was hungry at the time. As the firstborn, he should have been the one to bring forth the Messiah, but Esau messed up from the start, leaving his tricky, yet obedient brother, Jacob, to take his place.

It cannot be said enough. God loves obedience from His children. John, one of the sons of thunder, was called the disciple whom Jesus loves. This is because John was one of his closest and most obedient disciples. He stayed close to Jesus at supper and even leaned on him sometimes as he taught. John found delight in his Master and could barely separate himself from Him.

Today, let us give ourselves over to God's will. Study His word. Do the things He desires of us, like feeding the poor, loving our neighbours or esteeming others better than ourselves. By doing so, He will love us and manifest Himself to us. Without a shadow of a doubt, the disciple whom Jesus loves is the one who chooses to obey God and keep his statutes.

Let's pray: *Father, help me to be an obedient disciple like Jacob and John, fit for Your kingdom, in Jesus' holy name, Amen.*

Notes

Day 37 - No Retreat, No Surrender!

Scripture: *⁶So built we the wall; and all the wall was joined together unto the half thereof: for the people had a mind to work.* Nehemiah 4:6

Have you ever found yourself in a situation where you were thinking of trying something new, and decided to share it with friends? You were probably expecting them to cheer you on, but instead, you were met with peels of laughter. The idea sounded great to you at the time, yet their reactions left you wondering if you were losing your mind.

I admit, it's not the greatest feeling in the world to have friends or family dismiss your vision. Some of us may have had a nice, long pity party privately over it. Still, there is good to come from this. The experience gives us insight into who the people around us really are, but more importantly, it gives the opportunity to do something extraordinary. Something that everyone thought you couldn't do.

If God has put a burden on your heart to do a specific work for His glory, never allow Satan to use negative people around you to get you distracted from God's directive. The naysayers, like Sanballat and Tobiah, may have spoken evil against your plans even before they began. But if God has decreed it, then nothing can stop it from coming to pass.

The enemy's bark is greater than his bite, I promise you. He uses naysayers to discourage you from accomplishing the task God gave you to do, but my encouragement to you today is this. Set your face as flint against the enemy. Pick up your weapon in one hand (the armour of God) and fight while you work. Retreating is not an option. Surrendering is not an option. Just know that God is with you every step of the way. He will never leave you to fight on your own.

Let's pray: *Lord Jesus, give us Your strength to fight in the battle ahead. No retreat, no surrender, in Jesus' name, Amen.*

Notes

Day 38 - Iron-Clad Contract

Scripture: [30]*When Jesus therefore had received the vinegar, he said, It is finished: and he bowed his head, and gave up the ghost.* John 19:30

Signatures are powerful. They are our unique mark of identity that separates us from billions of other people on earth. No two signatures are the same, even in the case of forgery. Like your fingerprint, your signature is exclusive to you and where you put it can alter the course of your life, as well as the lives of others. Over the years, we've seen contracts being signed between governments, marking their countries' independence, or bills of rights or even peace treaties. Our signatures seal contractual agreements either temporarily or permanently.

After the fall of man, God made a promise to Eve and the serpent. He was going to put enmity between them. Over time, we learned that this animosity was going to lead to either destruction or sacrifice. In the end, God chose sacrifice. He made an everlasting covenant with Abraham that could not be broken. It was through this covenant that we gained that holy child, Jesus, who would become the firstborn among many brethren. Jesus' declaration on the cross, "It is finished," was His permanent signature that we were no longer owned by death and destruction, but were redeemed through His sacrifice.

This is an iron-clad contract that cannot be broken. At least, not on the part of our Lord. He has already done His part. Now it is time for us to seal the deal permanently. For God I live, for God I die. Many Christians are not ready to die for Him, but Jesus said in Luke 9:62, "No man, having put his hand to the plough, and looking back, is fit for the kingdom of God." Just as Jesus gave His all for our salvation, we must give our all for Him.

Let's pray: *Lord Jesus, thank You for dying on the cross to save us from our sins. Today we seal the deal by living for You unashamedly and without reservation, in Jesus' name, Amen.*

Notes

Day 39 - Nothing of his in Me

Scripture: [30]*Hereafter I will not talk much with you: for the prince of this world cometh, and hath nothing in me.* John 14:30

I never grew up with my mother. For a long time, my father's side of the family was all I knew. As could be said of any other household, there was no doubt that we were related. Many of us sounded alike, to the point where people sometimes couldn't tell the difference. We also looked alike, sometimes even laughed alike. Still, there were things about me that didn't quite fit in with my father's kin, and it was only years later when I reconnected with my mother that I got the full picture of who I was. The genes just can't lie!

For a while, Adam and Eve held God's identity. However, after Eve allowed herself to be deceived, and Adam decided to follow in her wake and sin against God, something foreign entered them and changed them, thereby sealing their new reality. They were suddenly sinful creatures, far away from God and in need of salvation. Unfortunately, as time went by, mankind became more and more like the devil, choosing to do evil rather than good.

Thankfully, Jesus Christ (the second Adam) came and changed the trajectory of our future. He testified in John 14:30 that the prince of this world (Satan), had nothing of his in Him. Jesus and Satan were as opposite as opposites could be, and with His sacrifice on the cross, we now have the ability to reject the evil in us and choose the good. If you have received salvation (Acts 2:38), then you have, of course, chosen the good. As we allow the Holy Spirit to train our spirit, we become like Jesus, and can finally say, "There is nothing of Satan's in me." Through the regeneration of the Holy Ghost, we are made new. We are made righteous. We are made holy. We are made free.

Let's pray: *Lord Jesus, thank You for dying for us and restoring us to our place as sons of God, in Jesus' name, Amen.*

Notes

Day 40 – What's Your Passion?

Scripture: [24]*And they that are Christ's have crucified the flesh with the affections and lusts.* Galatians 5:24

I've decided to close the way I began; by tackling the same question from day one: What's your passion? Perhaps, like me, at the beginning of this reset, you were worn out, exhausted and lacked the driving passion needed to take you to that higher place in God. Possibly that's why you got this book in the first place. To revive that craving for the things of God.

The trials and cares of this life, mixed with the rapid converting of this world into deeper, more sinister wickedness, can and will take a toll on any believer's spiritual walk with God. This is why we should take the time out to pull away from everything and lock ourselves in with the Lord. Today, I want you to reevaluate yourself. How has your walk been with Christ since the beginning of this reset? Have you been praying? Have you fasted at all? Have you read your Bible? Have you regained that deep, all-consuming love and passion you once had for God?

Putting our fleshly desires under subjection and choosing Jesus Christ does not come easy or natural, due to our sinful nature. All the same, we must make it our daily routine to put our flesh under subjection and choose God. As we discussed on Day 1, King David made many mistakes in his life, but he never allowed his failures to separate him from God. He always returned to his God, crawling hands and knees after Him.

If you've found yourself unable to retrieve this passion for God, start again. Dig deeper. Find Him. He promises that He will be found if you search for Him with all your heart! And for those of us who have found our passion in Christ, let's help someone else to find their way.

Let's pray: *Father, thank You for these forty days of prayer, fasting and Bible reading. You have helped me to rediscover my passion in You, and I am forever grateful, in Jesus' name, Amen.*

Notes

About the Author

IEASHA M POWELL is an accomplished author and ghostwriter with over a decade of experience writing professionally. Her main focus is on Christian Fiction and Non-Fiction. She has built a reputation for delivering compelling narratives that inspire and uplift readers in all walks of life. Her debut novel, A Crime for a Crown, was published in 2018.

As a ghostwriter, Ieasha has collaborated with dozens of clients, many established authors themselves, helping them bring their visions to life and consistently exceeding their expectations. Writing is not just her profession but her passion and God-given talent, allowing her to share messages of faith, redemption, and hope. It must be said that she also enjoys a good, clean, Hallmark-type romance novel, even without Christian themes in them. After all, good writing is just that - good writing!

When she's not writing, Ieasha enjoys reading, watching documentaries and engaging in enriching biblical discussions with her husband, Chris. Through her work, Ieasha seeks to not only entertain but also inspire readers to deepen their spiritual journey with the Lord Jesus. 40 Days to Spiritual Reset is one of her tools to achieve this. You can learn more about her at kissmypen.com.

Also by Ieasha:

Debut Novel - A Crime for a Crown
Available on Kobo Books App

A life of slavery is all that Suzanna Hayles has ever known or been exposed to. But the tragic murder of a fellow-servant, a boy she happens to have very strong feelings for, sends her and her father on a run for their lives, when they are accused of committing the crime.

And just when she thought things could not get any worse, Suzanna loses her father by the hands of a group of bandits in an unfamiliar territory. She must escape before they rape and kill her. The only way to do that is to find the castle of Lord Darvon, King of Albania. Suzanna is sure he is old and grumpy, until she beholds the face of the king.

Lord Darvon is the most miserable man alive. Having lost his wife and his unborn child, he is left wounded and depressed. The king has made up in his mind that he will never marry again. That is, until a green-eyed beauty barges into his castle battered and bruised.

Where to Follow:

Website: kissmypen.com

You can find all my links here:

https://linktr.ee/kissmypen

References:

1. Louden, Westcott (2021), Enlighten University: The Way of the Shaman, A Course.
Website: https://www.udemy.com/course/the-way-of-the-shaman-a-course/

2. Website: www.fiverr.com (catergories >> Spirtuality)

3. Ryrie, Charles Caldwell (1986, 1994) Ryrie King James Study Bible , English, King James Version

God Bless You!!!